Skin

Written by Pete Jenkins
Illustrated by Hazel Quintanilla

Rourke
Educational Media
rourkeeducationalmedia.com

Before & After Reading Activities

Teaching Focus:
Teacher-child conversations: Teacher-child conversations play an important role in shaping what children learn. Practice this and see how these conversations help scaffold your student's learning.

Before Reading:

Building Academic Vocabulary and Background Knowledge
Before reading a book, it is important to set the stage for your child or student by using pre-reading strategies. This will help them develop their vocabulary, increase their reading comprehension, and make connections across the curriculum.

1. Read the title and look at the cover. *Let's make predictions about what this book will be about.*
2. Take a picture walk by talking about the pictures/photographs in the book. Implant the vocabulary as you take the picture walk. Be sure to talk about the text features such as headings, the Table of Contents, glossary, bolded words, captions, charts/diagrams, or Index.
3. Have students read the first page of text with you then have students read the remaining text.
4. Strategy Talk – use to assist students while reading.
   - Get your mouth ready
   - Look at the picture
   - Think…does it make sense
   - Think…does it look right
   - Think…does it sound right
   - Chunk it – by looking for a part you know
5. Read it again.

Content Area Vocabulary
Use glossary words in a sentence.

bled
covers
crinkly
tone

After Reading:

Comprehension and Extension Activity
After reading the book, work on the following questions with your child or students in order to check their level of reading comprehension and content mastery.
1. What happens to your skin if you cut it or get hurt? (Summarize)
2. Why do you think people have different skin tones? (Asking Questions)
3. What does your skin cover? (Text to self connection)
4. When you get older, how does your skin change? (Asking Questions)

Extension Activity
Look at pictures in a magazine of people of all ages. Do you notice the different tones or how, depending on their age, their skin is different? Cut pictures out of all the different kinds of skin you see in the magazine. Glue them onto a piece of paper and have an adult help you label each picture. Some examples could be: dark skin, freckled skin, wrinkly skin, and smooth skin.

Table of Contents

My Skin 4

Stretchy Skin 8

Crinkly, Wrinkly Skin 16

Picture Glossary 23

About the Author 24

My Skin

I see my skin. It **covers** my bones.

I saw Lola's skin.

Her skin has a different tone.

7

Stretchy Skin

I see my skin. It stretches as I grow.

I saw Zac's skin.

He said, "How do you know?"

I see my skin.

In the sun, it turns red!

I saw Mariah's skin.

When she fell, it **bled**.

Crinkly, Wrinkly Skin

I see my skin. In the bathtub, it gets **crinkly.**

I saw Arthur's skin.

He said when you get old it gets wrinkly.

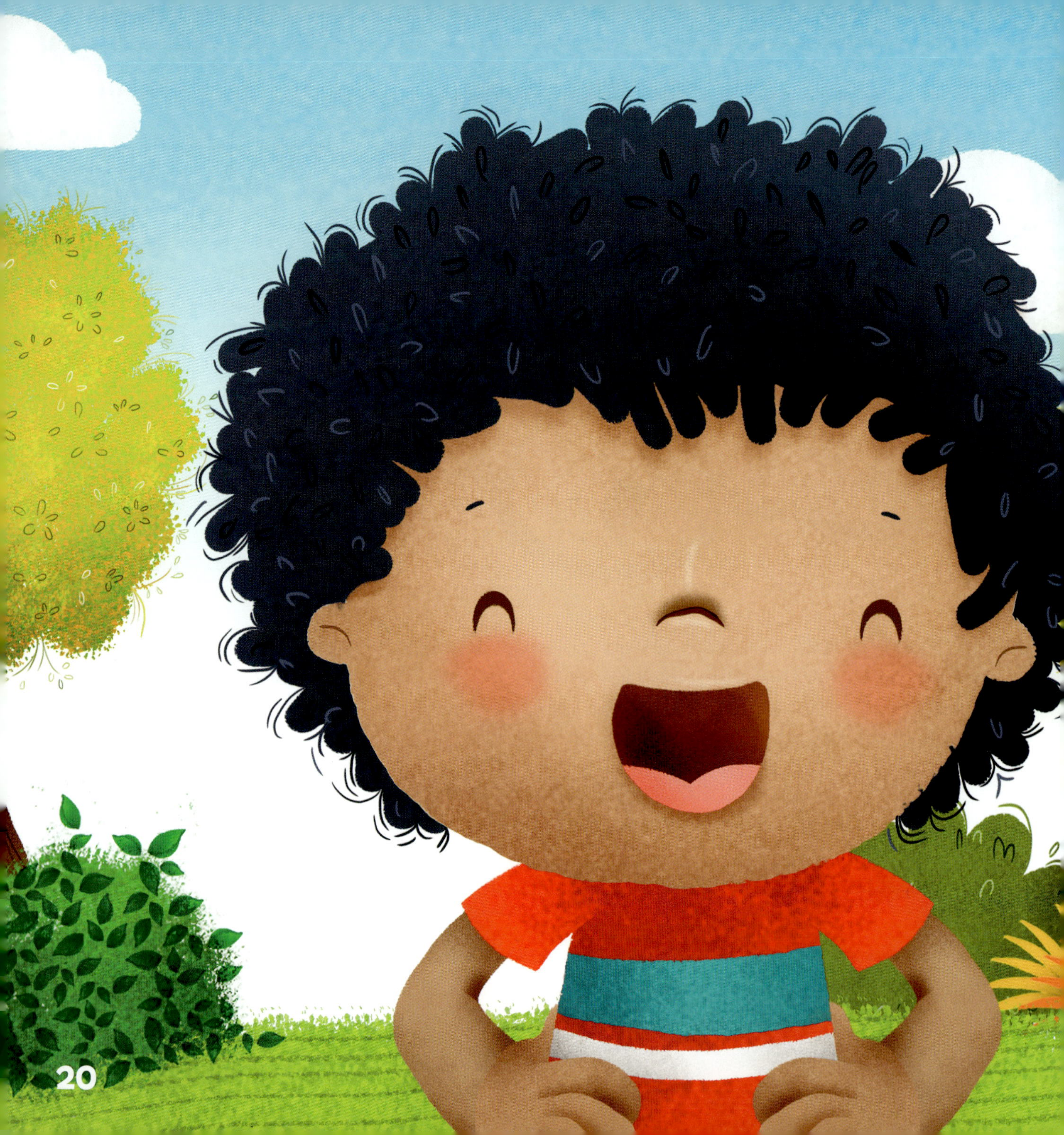

I see my skin. And it's ALL mine.

I love my skin!

Picture Glossary

bled (bled): If your skin has bled, it may have been injured by a cut or a fall.

covers (KUHV-urs): When something covers something else, it is draped over or on top of something, like your skin covers your bones.

crinkly (KRINGK-lee): When something is crinkly, it is full of creases or wrinkles.

tone (tohn): Tone is a hint or shade of a color. Everyone has a different skin tone.

About the Author

Pete Jenkins has a darker tone of skin. He lives in Florida, so when he goes to the beach it gets even darker. He loves his skin and always tries to protect it by wearing sunscreen. He doesn't want wrinkly skin when he gets older!

Meet The Author!
www.meetREMauthors.com

Library of Congress PCN Data

Skin/ Pete Jenkins
(I See, I Saw)
ISBN 978-1-68342-310-2 (hard cover)
ISBN 978-1-68342-406-2 (soft cover)
ISBN 978-1-68342-476-5 (e-Book)
Library of Congress Control Number: 2017931160

Rourke Educational Media
Printed in the United States of America,
North Mankato, Minnesota

© 2018 Rourke Educational Media

All rights reserved. No part of this book may be reproduced or utilized in any form or by any means, electronic or mechanical including photocopying, recording, or by any information storage and retrieval system without permission in writing from the publisher.

www.rourkeeducationalmedia.com

Edited by: Keli Sipperley
Cover and interior illustrations by: Hazel Quintanilla
Page layout by: Kathy Walsh